HOT and COLD

Nicolas Brasch

Nelson Thornes

Nelson Thornes

First published in 2007 by Cengage Learning Australia
www.cengage.com.au

This edition published in 2008 under the imprint of Nelson Thornes Ltd,
Delta Place, 27 Bath Road, Cheltenham, United Kingdom, GL53 7TH

10 9 8 7 6 5 4 3 2
11 10 09 08

Hot and Cold
ISBN 978-1-4085-0070-5

Text by Nicolas Brasch
Illustrations by Boris Silvestri
Edited by Johanna Rohan
Designed by James Lowe
Series Design by James Lowe
Production Controller Hanako Smith
Photo Research by Corrina Tauschke
Audio recordings by Juliet Hill, Picture Start
Spoken by Matthew King and Abbe Holmes
Printed in China by 1010 Printing International Ltd

Website www.nelsonthornes.com

Acknowledgements
The author and publisher would like to acknowledge permission to reproduce material from
the following sources:
Photographs by APL/Corbis/Robert Weight/Ecoscene, p. 15; Lindsay Edwards, back cover, pp. 4-5; Photo
Edit/David Young-Wolff, p. 11; Photolibrary.com/Rick Price, pp. 10, 13/ Superstock, Inc., p. 10 inset/
Photolibrary.com/Age foto stock/Frank Krahmer, p. 12/ Photolibrary.com/Science Photo Library/Doug
Allan, cover bottom.

HOT and COLD

Nicolas Brasch

Contents

Chapter 1

WHAT IS TEMPERATURE?

Temperature is the measure of how hot or cold something is.

Some people look at the TV to hear the air temperature.

Some people go outside to see if it is hot or cold.

Temperature is measured on a scale.

There are two scales:
Celsius and **Fahrenheit**.

The Celsius scale is named
after a man called Celsius.
He lived from 1701–1744.

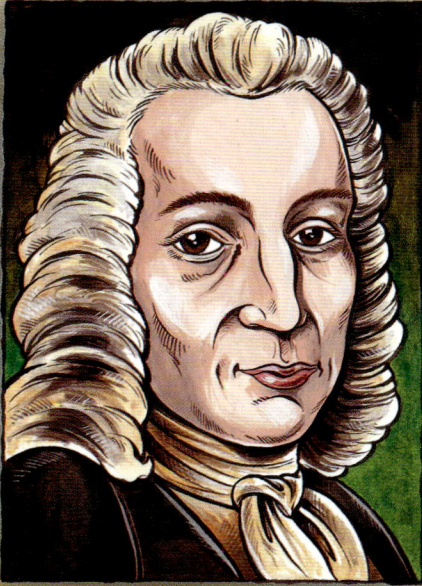

Anders Celsius

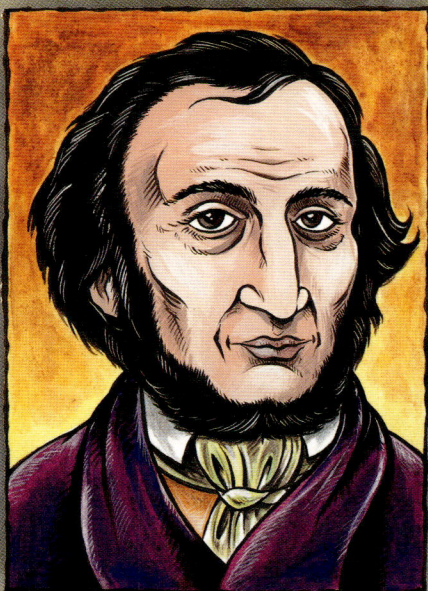

Daniel Fahrenheit

The Fahrenheit scale is named after a man called Fahrenheit. He lived from 1686–1736.

Some countries use the Celsius scale to measure temperature. Some countries use the Fahrenheit scale to measure temperature.

Chapter 2

MEASURING TEMPERATURE

This is a **thermometer**.

A thermometer measures the temperature.

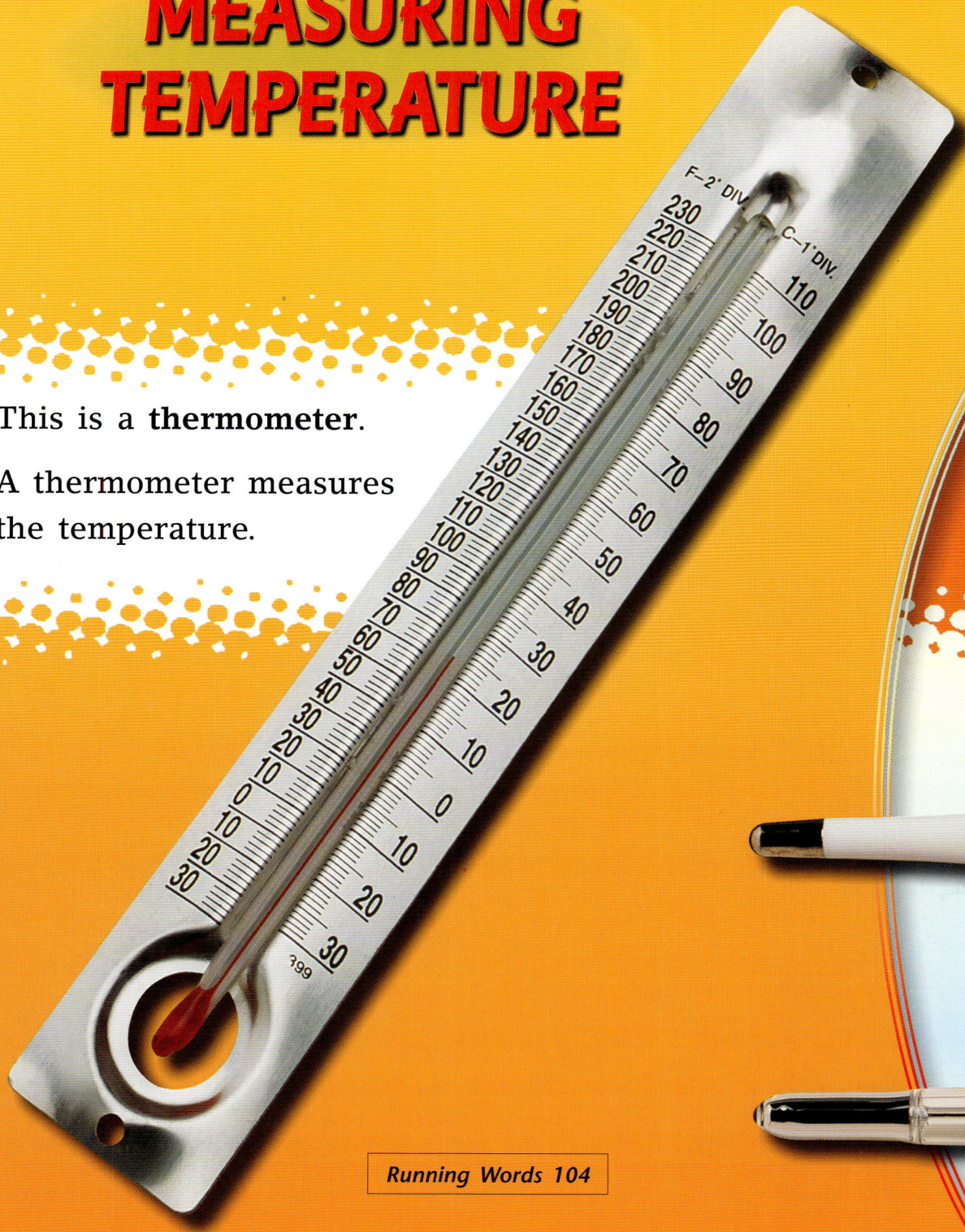

Running Words 104

The numbers on the thermometer are called **degrees**.
This is the sign for degree: °
All countries use 'degrees'
when talking about temperature.

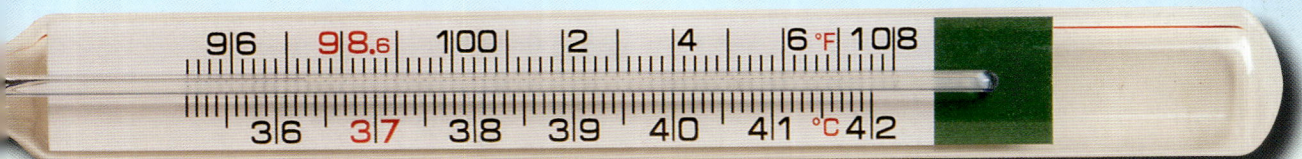

On the Celsius scale, water freezes at 0°.
On the Fahrenheit scale, water freezes at 32°.

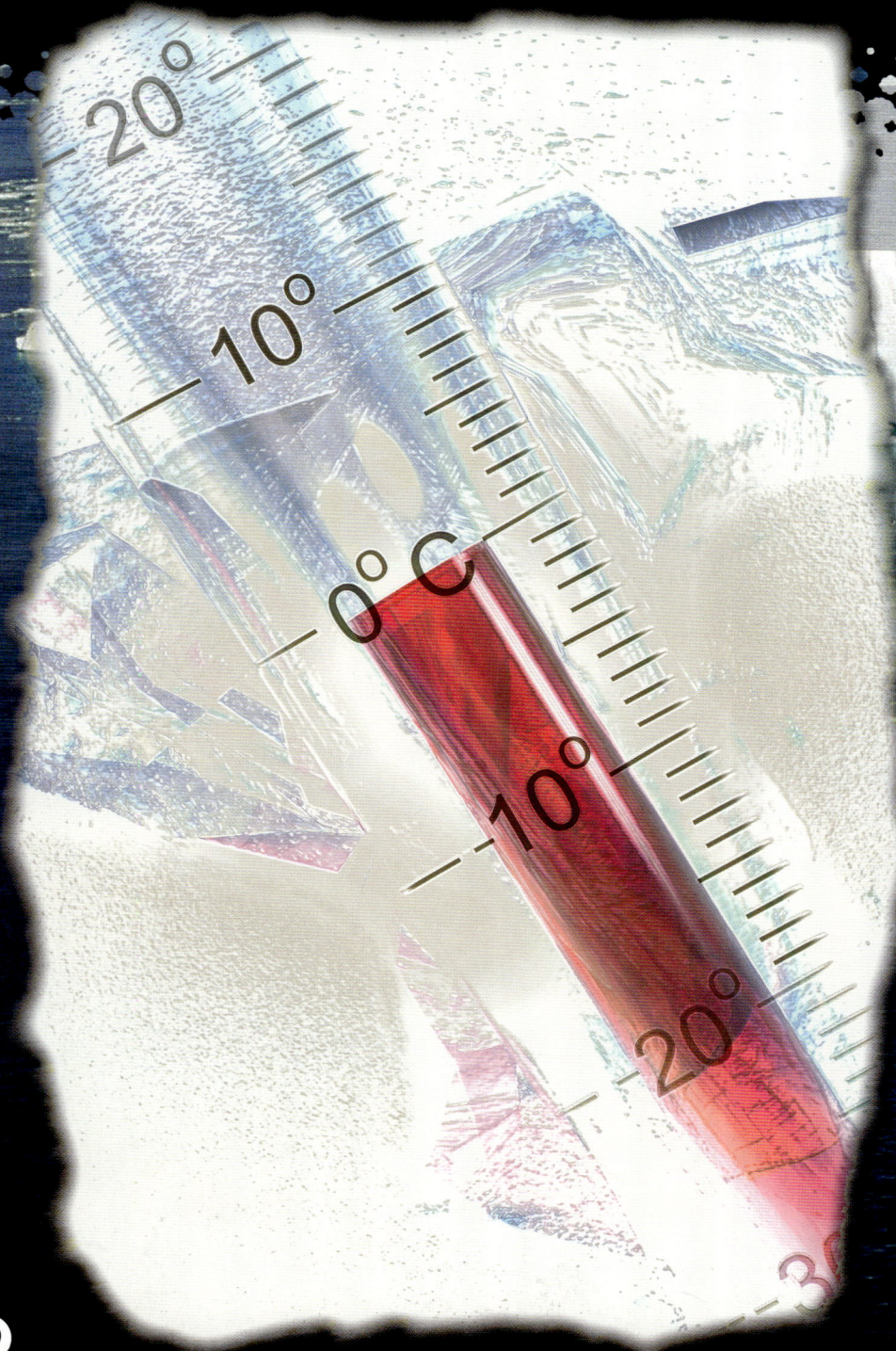

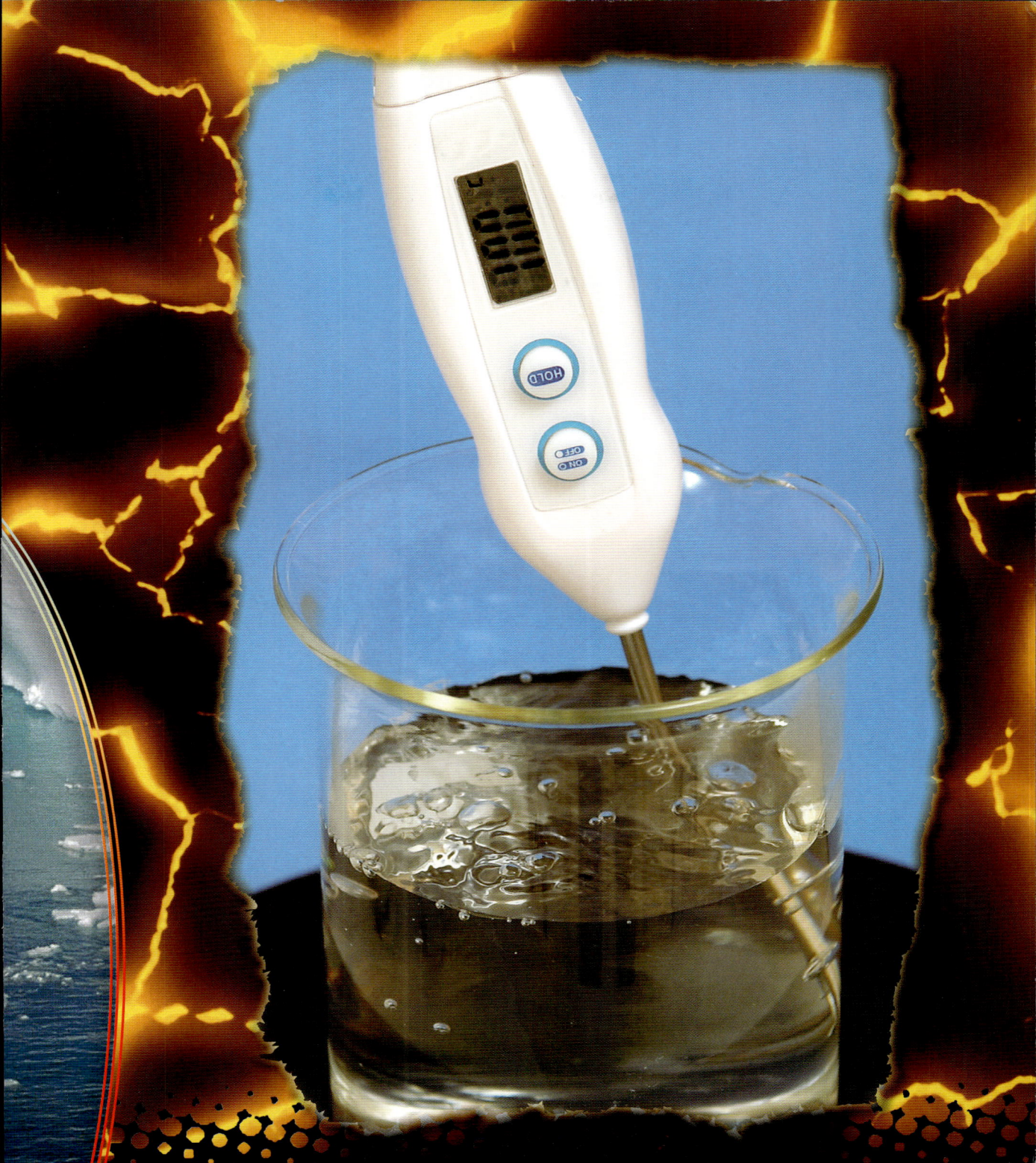

On the Celsius scale, water boils at 100°.
On the Fahrenheit scale, water boils at 212°.

Chapter 3

HOT AND COLD DAYS

Most parts of the world are hot for some of the year and cold for some of the year.

Some parts of the world are hot all of the year. Libya is hot all of the year.

Some parts of the world are cold all of the year.
Antarctica is cold all of the year.

On 13 September 1922, a temperature of 57.3°C (136°F) was measured in Libya.
This is the hottest temperature measured in a country.

Libya

Antarctica

On 21 July 1983, a temperature of -89.2°C (-128.6°F) was measured in Antarctica.
This is the coldest temperature measured on Earth.

Vostock station in Antarctica

Temperature Facts

The hottest temperature measured in Australia is 50.0°C (122°F).

The coldest temperature measured in Australia is -23.0°C (-9.4°F).

The hottest temperature measured in the USA is 56.7°C (134°F).

The coldest temperature measured in the USA is -62.1°C (-79.8°F).

Glossary

Celsius   a scale to measure temperature. Water freezes at 0° Celsius.

degrees   units of measurement on a thermometer

Fahrenheit   a scale to measure temperature. Water freezes at 32° Fahrenheit.

temperature   how hot or cold something is

thermometer   an instrument that measures temperature

Index